Daughters,
Not a Curse

DAUGHTERS, Not a Curse

A BOOK OF POETRY

BY
ANILA BUKHARI

© 2024 Daughters Not a Curse
Written by: Anila Bukhari
Edited by: Brandy Lane
Associate Editor: Kelsey Annin
Formatted by Brandy Lane

All rights reserved.
Printed in the United States of America.

No part of this book may be used, stored in a system retrieval system, or transmitted, in any form or any means—by electronic, mechanical, photocopying, recording, or reproduced in any manner whatsoever—without written permission from the author, except in the case of brief quotations embodied in critical articles and reviews.

Published in the United States of America by
Where Beautiful Inks LLC
Fort Wayne, Indiana

ISBN: 978-1-7363268-8-6

Library of Congress Control Number: 2024906911

Cover portrait of child done by: Bashir Muslim
Cover Design by Brandy Lane
All other images throughout this book are available through Canva and Canva Pro.

Dedication

To my sweetest mom,

Daughters, Not a Curse is a book dedicated to you, the woman who has been my constant inspiration and unwavering support. You have fearlessly fought against social norms to ensure I receive the rights and opportunities I deserve as your daughter.

Your love, guidance, and sacrifices have been a true blessing in my life. You have shown me that daughters are not curses but extraordinary gifts that have the power to change the world.

Thank you for standing by my side, believing in me, and being the epitome of strength and resilience. This book is a tribute to your unwavering love and the countless ways you have shaped my journey.

I dedicate this book with all my love and gratitude.

Your daughter,
Anila Bukhari

I love you Mom

Preface

Dear Readers,

In this world where girls are often confined by societal norms, it's time to break free from those cages and embrace the power within. My book, "Daughters Not a Curse," is a heartfelt collection of verses that aims to empower and uplift girls who have been made to believe they are less than. It challenges the notion that the birth of daughters is a curse and instead celebrates their strength and potential.

Regardless of our religious beliefs, the message remains the same: daughters deserve love, care, and respect. In this book, I draw inspiration from the wisdom of Prophet Muhammad, who emphasized the importance of women's rights and their immense value.

Join me on this poetic journey as we celebrate the resilience of girls and work towards a society where daughters are cherished and their potential is recognized. Together, let's rewrite the narrative and create a brighter future where every girl is seen as a blessing.

Tons of Love,

Anila Bukhari

Foreword

Friends,

It is not often that you come across such a passion for humanity in someone as young as Anila Bukhari. Her depth of empathy for others is astounding and very much alive through her poetry. We mustn't take for granted the privileges we have, where we reside, and the freedoms that we have, because not everyone has those same luxuries.

That is not the way it should be. Freedom should not be a luxury. It should be a way of life. It should be part of the experience of simply being human. Men and women of all races, religions, and creeds should all be allowed to share the same basic human rights, but unfortunately, the world is disjointed. We are not as one, although we all breathe the same air, walk in the same rain, and all have the same needs.

Anila is brave in sharing her words, as any woman is when we show our true colors. We want to be heard, respected and allowed the same successes as everyone else. I sincerely hope that, either as a woman or a burgeoning one, you will be uplifted and empowered by the words within these pages. If you happen to be a man reading these words, I pray you find compassion, respect, and humbleness in them. May you find understanding for the feminine and see the strength that makes all women invaluable.

In love and light,
Brandy Lane

Contents

Don't Break Our Hearts 2

A Bloodless, Coronary Heart 3

Oh, Rose! Open Your Heart 4

Rain, Rain, Remove My Sorrow 5

My Last Wish 6

Wish of A Girl 7

Different Heart 8

Give Greetings to My Amazing God 9

My True Worth 10

I'm Singing My Song of Grief 12

My Connection With My God 14

Sad Mother 16

Day Dreamer 18

Forgive My Dear Heart 20

Cruel Reminder 22

Song of Tears 24

Heavy Soul 26

Goodbye, My Dear Pet Friend 27

Lovely Soul 28

Tears Fall Like Rain 30

Sorrow And Pain 32

I Pray For Peace 34

She Is Like A Star 35

Moon Beauty 36

Day of Judgement 38

God Is Always With You 40

I Lost My Heart 42

Memories 43

Thank You, God 44

Believe 45

Black Women 46

True Happiness 48

A Painful Moment 49

Morning Light 50

My Soul's Secret 52

Portrait by Bashir Muslim

DAUGHTERS, Not a Curse

A BOOK OF POETRY

Anila Bukhari

Don't Break Our Hearts

Daughters, not a curse, but a divine blessing.
Mommy, please do not ruin our hearts; let our spirits shine.
We aren't inferior or lesser than your sons.
We too, have passions and desires to be won.

Please allow us and grant us our rights.
Let our voices soar and reach new heights.
In this vast world, we are seeking equality—
to break free from the chains of patriarchy.

As daughters, we are strong—and full of grace,
with minds that dream and hearts that embrace.
We are seeking education to gain—
knowledge and prove that our worth isn't in vain.

For too long, we have been silenced and oppressed,
but now we rise, determined to address
the injustice that holds us back.
With courage and resilience, we will stay on track.

Let us choose our own destiny—our own path—
for we have dreams and aspirations that won't fade to black.
We'll break barriers and shatter glass ceilings
with our determination and inner healings.

Daughters, not a curse, but a pure blessing.
Let us rise, and let our voices be heard.
Mommy, please don't break our hearts; set them free.
For we are destined to be all that we can be.

A Bloodless, Coronary Heart

I wonder why God permits suffering;
why do humans hurt me and tear me apart inside?
Why do humans depress my spirit?
It comes from out of nowhere and feels so low.

Why is my heart aching
when all I crave is for love to be returned?
Why is my life not an area to love?
I was left cold and unhappy when he rejected my heart.

I want to be cold-hearted, truly.
I may not revel in rejection, so I may not revel in blue.
Those who reject my loyalty and belief
strike and snigger while I wallow in grief.

What is wrong with crying all the time?
What causes my coronary heart to bleed constantly?
Perhaps it's miles—the distance is cruel and unkind
or something internal to me, deep in my thoughts.

I am trying to find consolation and peace,
to convey my sweet freedom with a loving kiss.
I long for a place to which I can belong,
to mend my brokenness and heal what went wrong.

Though the ache lasts, so do the tears.
I rise high; I stand tall.
However shocking this suffering is,
I will go forth, resilient and adventurous.

Therefore, I will take on the struggles, accidents, and conflicts,
because they shape my adventure and my future.
Even though my coronary heart feels aching,
I see the beauty that ache can deliver.

ANILA BUKHARI

Oh, Rose! Open Your Heart

Yeah, this is me.
I'm seeking a place where no one returns, you see.
A city of the unknown, a world unseen,
Alone in gathering, yet with many in my lineless dream.

Who am I? The answer eludes.
I'm brave as an eagle and polite as a bird's heart in my attributes.
Like a leaf on a tree, I sway.
Alone: draped in the shawl of loneliness, day by day.

Who am I? I still don't know.
Oh, Rain! Oh, Moon! Be my friend, and let your presence show.
Many people love my aim,
but finding someone who accepts all of me,
both the good and the bad, remains the game.

Who understands my sorrow, my tears, and my nature?
When will I find a soul close to me, a kindred creature?
This world is filled with people, it's true,
but finding a true lover—oh! What a journey to pursue.

Oh, Cloud! Embrace me, and let me hide within your embrace,
Oh, Rose! Open your heart and grant me solace in your grace.
In your beauty, I wish to find peace.
For in your embrace, I yearn for my release.

Rain, Rain Remove My Sorrow

Oh, Rain, stay close to me.
I adore you. Can you not see?
Your touch on my body is so light
and makes my hair dance in the breeze. Oh, what a sight!

I love walking the streets at sundown's hour,
watching the moon's reflection on the lake with power.
Rain, my dear, protect me from this sorrow and pain.
Please wash away my troubles and let peace reign.

Listen to my voice, Rain! I'm all alone.
Remove this loneliness and make my heart known.
I thirst for love! Let it fill me inside,
With every drop of yours, may my pain subside.

The intoxicating scent of rain on dry earth is oh-so-sweet!
As I walk in the rain—a peaceful retreat—
to a place where no one can hurt or reject you.
With simplicity and loyalty that I can connect to.

Remember, Rain, one day I'll be gone,
leaving behind memories—like a distant song.
Yet, your essence will remain forever in my heart,
a reminder of the peace and healing you impart.

Rain, Rain, remove my sorrow.
Bring me joy today and tomorrow.

ANILA BUKHARI

My Last Wish

Though I might also leave at some point,
I'll still see paradise in a chic vision.
Grant me the desire to be a shoulder for those in need
and a comforting wipe for those whose tears flow free.

Let there be a sweet corner in your heart
for the orphaned and lonely.
I do not ask for visits to my grave
or for tears to be sown forever and ever.

Instead, I implore you to share a smile
with those who have lost their way,
For difficult lives have stolen their joy
while leaving them in chaos.

Offer a bouquet of roses to people
who long for a touch of care.
To those who have nobody,
let them know that someone's there.

Wish of a Girl

In a humble home of dust and clay
lives a young girl with a heart full of play.
She spends her days in the company of animals
and finds solace in their gentle rhythms.

Her eyes sparkle with a desire to see
beyond the limits of her humble stage.
Social norms bound her wings,
preventing her from spreading them and flying.

She cries into her grandmother's pillow
as she wishes for a world that is more than just hollow.
She longs to be a shining star,
but the weight of tradition holds her back.

She writes her wishes in the dirt
and hopes for a future that is not dirt.
Peace evades her grasp
as she struggles to break free from the past.

Different Heart

I am a common girl like you
but with a unique heart,
I wonder why I must go through
trials that seem to begin differently.
Why do I complain and plead
when God has accomplished His will?
Why do I bleed and weep
when He has given me His talent?

I shed a hundred layers
of impurity before my Lord.
Then I understand His uniqueness
and His responsibility to shape.

He answers yes or no.
He gives not what I want,
but what is best for me to grow,
and what will cause me to desire.

He is my light in the darkest night.
He wants me higher than a mountain's top.
He gives me trouble and pain
to make me a leader like an eagle's flight.

Just like gold that burns in fire,
I become more beautiful than before.
Just like a rose that suffers pain,
I become a flower that is more than just a flower.

Let us be content with God's will.
Let us believe in His plan for us all.
For He knows what is best for us still,
and He will make us stand tall.

Give Greetings to My Amazing God

In fields of sunflowers, a lady roams freely.
With her flowing hair, she stands in awe.
She's plucking cotton delicately from the earth
as she cradles it in her pure palm.

With a gentle breath
and white dance against the sky,
the cotton takes flight,

Her voice carries through the fields
as she sings praises to the heavens above.
"Oh, Cotton, you resemble an antique woman!
With silvery tresses, bring greetings to my beloved God,"
she serenades with passion.

Sunflowers sway in harmony
as their vibrant petals join the dance.

In her own crafted stanza, she reaches for the sky
with her arms outstretched in a graceful rhythm.

"Give my greetings to my exceptional God,
the one who loves and cares for eternity.
I am grateful for the pain that has shaped me into an artist,
and for the challenging days and nights
that is birthing a brand-new life within me."

Tears blend with smiles, a testament to the journey she's embraced.
"Oh, my extraordinary God, you have granted me the power of prayer,
ignited the fire of passion within me,
and blessed me with a mind and body that are forever grateful.
Give my greetings to my great God,
the one who embraces all regardless of mistakes or skin type
and is always present in the nights and days."

ANILA BUKHARI

My True Worth

My heart feels heavy from a friend I knew,
The bond we shared is now damaged. Oh, what do I do?
The one I trusted, my true confidant,
has harmed me with words of malintent.

Why do I mourn for one who is unkind?
Whose praises for me I never did find?
Who never cared after I wanted a friend,
who rejected me over and over again.

They bruised my joy and my self-respect, too.
In their eyes, I am nothing but a fool.
They see me as thirsty for status and wealth,
but don't they know I'm as natural as water, myself?

I was there for care, love, and remedy,
but they saw me as someone else. Oh, what a theory!
I am viewed as a girl just searching for a man and his money,
but my intentions were pure. Oh, how very funny!

I lost everything when I met this friend,
but money was not the biggest loss in the end.
The real loss was the one I held dear,
the one who was near, and the one I held close to.

Why do I weep for those who don't care?
For those who never saw my smile, so rare?
They're too busy with their new girlfriends,
leaving me behind in tears and sad ends.

Now I've decided to break away
from this poisonous friendship that led me astray.
My success will show how worthy I am
and how valuable I was to them.

I've received love from all over the world,
but my careless friend never saw my worth unfurled.
They were always looking for something more
and left me for a shallow life so sore.

Now I rise from the ashes of pain.
I'll never let someone hurt me again.
I've learned my lesson from this harmful friend,
and now I know my true worth in the end.

ANILA BUKHARI

I'm Singing My Song of Grief

The track of grief echoes from my heart
as I ask for forgiveness from the start.
I'm sorry if I caused you any harm or pain.
I hope you can forgive me, or it's all in vain.

I regret I couldn't visit you—
or let you know when my time was due.
When I pass away and lay in my grave,
I hope you might come and visit; be brave.

In life, no one cared for me.
It's a sad reality for all to see.
No one held me in their loving arms.
No one showed me their love and charms.

Today, the burden on my heart is heavy.
Friendship seems to be nothing but petty.
People are fake and so very cruel.
While sweet on the surface, deep down they rule.

Grief, you've been my eternal companion since my birth.
Happiness is my enemy that's never on earth,
I have no one to call my friend.
My heart shattered into pieces and will never mend.

Here I am singing my song of grief
from the bottom of my heart with disbelief.
For all the hurt and pain they have brought,
and for all the love and care I have not yet got.

Forgive me, for God's sake, if I hurt you,
In this world, friendships are so few.
However, in my grave, I'll wait for you,
for love and friendship, tried and true.

ANILA BUKHARI

My Connection With My God

I was once a baby without emotions
or connection to my God in the wild.
During my father's near-death, I prayed in despair,
but no one asked me to pray.

Deep in my heart, something was stirring.
A call sounds from my Creator, along with a divine urging.
Day by day, I feel a strong connection;
pain, grief, and suffering still touch my soul.

In my darkest moments, when pain hurts me,
I find solace in Allah, my Creator, my deity,
I feel closer to Him with every tear.
I know His presence. His mercy. His care.

I try to accept my saddest days
as Allah's will—in mysterious ways.
Though it breaks me like a painful trial,
He always gives me the strength to smile.

In every new ache, I turn to Him.
My best friend, in whom I confide and dream,
I'll share my sorrows, my struggles, and my fears.
He is the only one who wipes away my tears.

No matter how tough life can be,
through every trial, He teaches me,
True faith lies in trusting His plan,
even when it is hard to understand.

Every night, I pray with tears in my eyes,
and sometimes they touch my shirt—soaked with cries.
I pour out my broken story to God.
He heals me, comforts me, and guides me with His nod.

Through His grace, I find the strength to carry on.
Despite my battles, I rise with each sunrise—
for I am a believer with a faith so strong.
In my connection with My Creator—I find my lifelong song.

ANILA BUKHARI

Sad Mother

Once I had a son so handsome and kind;
He was stolen and taken in the blink of an eye.
He was taken from me by a cruel and cold-hearted person,
and now my world is filled with an indescribable darkness.

My heart aches for the son I cannot find,
who's lost in a world that is unkind.
Whenever his memory floods my mind,
my body breaks, and my soul lags behind.

His white shirt and watch live as little reminders,
and they only serve to intensify my pain.
For every moment without him feels like I'm restrained,
and my heart longs for him to come back to me, his guiding light.

The days go by, but I cannot move forward
without my son, my light, my precious one.
The people around me seem to have withdrawn,
unable to see my pain with hearts like stone.

I want to cry out in every city and town—
for my son, my love, and my lost crown.
Nobody seems to listen to even a sound,
and I wonder if they have all gone deaf or just indifferent.

I pray every day to whoever can hear
to bring my son back and wipe away my tears.
For this pain is too much, too heavy to bear,
and I beg, "Please stop this! Have mercy! Hear my plea!"

Until then, I'll keep searching and hoping
that one day my son will return, no more coping—
that my world will again be filled with light and no more groping.
For my son, my love is my everything. My world will stop mourning.

ANILA BUKHARI

Day Dreamer

She was a beautiful lady, so young and truthful—
a lady whose desires were more than simply thin air.
Every night, as she closed her eyes,
her visions take her to the skies.

She sees her destiny, vivid and clear,
and her life, filled with love, as nothing to fear.
From the age of ten until she turned thirty—
her dreams came true; it was quite a journey!

She saw special moments, both big and small.
In her dreams, she is living them all.
Amidst the joy, there was a dark theme,
for she also saw things she wished were just a dream.

One night, she saw a murder unfold;
a person's life was taken and left cold.
She woke up in fear with her heart racing fast,
but little did she know, this wouldn't be the last.

In her dreams she saw a boy;
and slowly but surely fell in love with joy.
Then, she saw signs of a disease,
and her heart shattered—as she fell to her knees.

She saw everything in her dreams so vividly,
but in reality, she was only a daydreamer and acted timidly.
She held big dreams she longed to fulfill,
like establishing a school for girls in Balochistan—such a thrill!

As she grew older, she faced failure,
and the dream of her school started to wither.
She never gave up; she held on tight.
She believed in her dream with all her might.

One day, her life was taken away
by terrorists who saw her as their only prey.
With her dreams, hopes, and life all cut short,
the world lost a dreamer of great worth.

Her legacy lives on in the hearts of many,
and her dream of a school became a reality.
Even in death, she continues to inspire and amaze.
Her beautiful name will forever be praised.

ANILA BUKHARI

Forgive My Dear Heart

Oh, my heart, how resilient you have been!
Through trials and pain, you still manage to grin.
My late-night talks are filled with advice,
still, you long for the sweet embrace of romance.

You give love to all you meet
but never receive—it's bittersweet.
Your uniqueness shines so bright;
forgive me, my dear heart, for my plight.

I know I've hurt you over and over,
but you never waver or bend.
You persevere through sorrow and grief
as I give myself away to those I meet.

I offer you to people, to my loved ones,
to social norms, and everyone inside.
Yet, they don't see your worth.
Dear heart, forgive me for this pain.

I promise you. I'll never give up;
for God knows your value and worth.
Of life's challenges, you've faced them all,
but still, you stand tall and never fall.

I want to live like a white butterfly,
or a nightingale soaring in the sky.
I'll speak and sing my song of joy
and even if no one hears, I'll never be coy.

My heart, you are my strength,
my guide, and my compass—my true friend.
I pray for your peace and your happiness,
and I'll never let you face loneliness.

Cruel Reminder

In Lahore, I saw a woman
whose face was disfigured by acid burns.
Her once vibrant eyes now filled with pain
as she struggled to survive each day in vain.

The scars on her skin serve as a cruel reminder
of a past she wished she could leave behind her.
However the people's mockery never ceased,
only adding to her pain and never granting her peace.

She refused to give up as her spirit shattered.
Her dreams were crushed, with her words left unspoken.
Her husband, once her protector, is now her enemy;
forcing her to live in a world of misery.

Her heart, once filled with love and light,
is now hidden in a dark and lonely night.
She dies inside a little more each day,
as she faces a world that treats her this way.

DAUGHTERS NOT A CURSE

I saw her in the hospital, a broken soul,
trying to hide the pain and stay whole.
Her eyes revealed the truth, and put her heart in despair
as she fought a battle she never wanted to bear.

In that moment my heart cried
for the woman whose spirit had died.
She will always remain in my memory
as a symbol of strength and bravery.

Even in the face of such cruelty,
she stood tall while never losing her dignity.
In Lahore, I saw a woman so resilient,
A woman whose story will forever live on.

ANILA BUKHARI

Song of Tears

Songs of tears drift ad infinitum
from the depths of my soul.
I'm afraid to leave this world behind
and lose everything I hold.

My heart is rather fearful
of the unknown that awaits.
Fear of leaving behind loved ones
and all that I create.

My siblings, my books, and my dreams
are all dear to my heart,
but most of all, my mama
whose love I cannot leave.

I am afraid to die,
to bid this world goodbye,
to leave behind my loved ones,
and to watch them as they cry.

My books, my escape,
my dreams, and my hope,
all give me the strength to carry on
in this vast, wide world.

DAUGHTER'S NOT A CURSE

Still, it's my mama's love
that keeps me going strong.
Her gentle touch and warm embrace
are where I truly belong.

I cannot bear the thought
of leaving her behind.
To face this world without her
is a pain I don't want to find.

So I'll hold on to this life
with every breath I take.
When my time has come
I'll leave without a mistake.

For though I'm afraid to die,
I know I'll be at peace
For I'll be reunited
with my loved ones, deceased.

And as I sing these songs of tears
I'll cherish every moment.
With my mama, my siblings,
and all that life has sent.

ANILA BUKHARI

Heavy Soul

My soul is heavy—my heart is pained,
for I have misplaced my beloved puppy, my friend.
His absence leaves a void, a constant ache,
and my tears fall like an endless rain.

I see his pictures, and my heart breaks;
he looks so sad—he misses me too.
I can't afford to bring him back,
and this reality, oh, how it makes me blue.

I long to hug him, to feel his fur,
and to cuddle him close and never let go.
My poverty keeps us apart,
and this reality hurts me so—.

He was my loyal companion,
my source of joy, my constant delight.
But now he is gone, and I am left
with nothing but memories and a heavy plight.

I pray for a miracle, for a change of fate—
to have him back in my arms once more.
Until then, my soul will keep crying
for losing my pet, whom I adore.

Goodbye, My Dear Pet Friend

My heart aches because my beloved pet is long gone.
I can't afford to keep him by my side.
The thought of him no longer in my home
leaves me with a feeling of emptiness inside.

He was more than just a furry companion.
He was my confidant, my best friend.
His presence brought such joy and happiness.
Now, it seems, all good things must come to an end.

I miss his wagging tail and loving eyes,
his playful barks and warm snuggles.
I know I can no longer provide
the food and care he so dearly needs.

So with a heavy heart, I made the decision
to give him to someone who could offer
all the things I couldn't afford.
Oh, how I cried.

I hope he finds a loving home
where he can be cherished and loved.
I know he will bring so much joy
to his new family, just as he did before.

My heart may still ache, but I find solace
in knowing he will be loved and well-fed.
Goodbye, my dear pet. I will always miss you,
but for your happiness, I will hold my head high instead.

Lovely Soul

She turned into a girl with a vengeance
to fight for what was right.
She raised her voice against the drugs
that was taking young lives out of sight.

But little did she realize
that her bravery would come at a cost.
The drug lords were not satisfied;
their earnings were going to be lost.

One day, as she walked home,
she was taken against her will.
Her captors—they were heartless,
and her heart—it stood quite still.

She was a lovely soul
with a kind and gentle heart.
Now, she was a prisoner,
torn apart from her life from the start.

She was a champion for women,
and their rights to be free,
but now, she was just a girl
trapped in a world of misery.

Her people searched for her;
but she was nowhere to be found.
They feared the worst had happened,
the heartbreak was profound.

Days turned into weeks
and weeks turned into months.
But still, there was no sign
of the girl who fought against drugs.

DAUGHTER'S NOT A CURSE

But she never gave up hope
for she knew her cause was just.
She prayed for supernatural strength
in the midst of this cruel unjust.

Finally, one day,
her captors were caught;
and she was let out—
her spirit—overwrought.

She returned to her people
with tears of joy and pain,
for she had been through hell,
but she was determined to remain—
a beacon of hope
for all the girls and boys.
She continued her fight
for their rights—and their joys.

Though her heart may have been broken,
and her spirit may have been bruised,
she rose above it all,
a true hero; she was proved.

So, let her be an inspiration
for all the girls out there;
even in the darkest times
we should never lose our care.

For a beautiful, kind heart
can withstand any pain.
In the end, it will triumph,
and peace and justice will reign.

ANILA BUKHARI

Tears Fall Like Rain

My heart is heavy and my tears fall like rain—
for the people who have lost someone and who feel the pain.
Their loved ones were taken, and their lives were cut too short.
How can I express my sorrow? My heart hurts as it contorts.

I weep for those who have been killed
and their families—their hearts left—unfulfilled.
I am not their relative, but my heart bleeds;
for the loss they have endured and for their shattered dreams.

My body—it feels empty. My soul— it knows the pain—
of a nation torn apart; our lives won't be the same.
How can I express myself, my inner grief, my sorrow—
for the gem that we have lost— hope for a brighter tomorrow?

But, I am bound by social norms.
My hands are tied; my voice isn't heard.
I long to speak—to cry out loud,
but my tongue is silent, and I'm not allowed.

DAUGHTER'S NOT A CURSE

My heart continues to mourn, and my soul feels sorrow
for a country that is lost for a better tomorrow.
I cannot attend the funeral; I cannot say goodbye—
but I pray for peace for the souls that have flown high.

Oh, angel, come to me in my dreams,
for in this world, nothing is as it seems.
You may be in paradise, but I am here—
weeping for our country—for those we hold dear.

My heart may be heavy, my tears may fall,
but I will not give up—I'll stand tall.
For one day, our country's gem will shine again,
and we'll be united in peace, not in pain.

ANILA BUKHARI

Sorrow And Pain

I saw a person, his lifeless shape,
laid out before my eyes.
His murder—a merciless injustice born.
And my heart—it wrenches and cries.

His wallet, his comb, his mirror too,
lay scattered on the ground.
Remnants of a life, now gone,
with no one there to make a sound.

His loved ones—his family,
filled with sorrow and pain.
Unable to raise awareness, unfortunately,
for their loved one, all in vain.

He was a brother, a son, a friend,
a man—who spoke for what was right.
But when it came to justice in the end—
the leaders of the nation stayed out of sight.

Silent they were—these so-called leaders,
turning a blind eye to the truth.
Their lack of action, like a poison feeder,
and justice left—without a proof.

It breaks my heart to see this scene
and to witness such a senseless loss.
For a man who stood for what was clean,
now left without a voice—no cause.

But let us not forget—his spirit lives on
in the hearts of those who fight.
For justice and truth, they will never be gone—
as long as we continue to shine their light.

So let us raise our voices aloud
for the man whose life was taken.
And let our cries spread like a cloud
until justice is no longer forsaken.

I Pray For Peace

My heart aches with sorrow and pain
when I see injustice and poverty reign.
The negative, downtrodden, and oppressed;
their cries and struggles—often suppressed.

I witnessed a mindless and cruel murder.
Innocent lives were taken, and my heart felt like an intruder.
Their blood spilled, staining the ground
and their memories untold, their voices—no longer found.

The photo of his wallet, filled with blood
haunts me like an endless flood.
The pockets he cherished, now a symbol of death
A reminder of the violence, of someone's final breath.

I saw a passionate individual, his eyes full of fire,
but now his life stolen, and his dreams have expired.
His reflection in his pocket is a reflection of his soul.
Now, he is gone, and his story—untold.

With a single shot, his life was taken;
leaving behind hearts—now forsaken.
I can't forget him; it tears me apart—
for he died unjustly, with a bullet in his heart.

My heart aches, my soul weeps—
for the lives lost, for the pain that now seeps.
Injustice and violence are a never-ending cycle;
leaving behind scars that are hard to stifle.

I pray for peace, for love to prevail,
and for innocent lives, and a story to tell.
But until then, my heart will always bear
the memories of those whose lives were taken unfairly.

She is Like A Star

A woman who fights with words instead of swords;
her life is in constant danger of death.
She continues to raise her voice
for the cause of women's education—with every breath.

People may hate her vision and despise her speech,
but she stands strong—with her pen as her weapon.
She knows the power of education
and the change it can bring to a true revolution.

She's seen fellow activists fall, taken by those who fear,
but it only fuels her fire to do even more.
She knows that her mission is greater than her fear—
and she'll keep fighting, even when her heart is sore.

She knows the value of sacrifice, of standing up for what's right,
but people merely offer condolences and then move on.
She's not afraid for she knows her purpose is worth the fight.
She'll continue to raise her voice until her final dawn.

She is like a star shining bright in the dark.
A beacon of hope for the oppressed and the vulnerable.
Like the sun rising every day, she'll make her mark.
Like flowers that bloom in the garden, she'll never be meek.

So, let her voice ring out, let her message be heard.
She fights not only for herself; but for every woman
who dreams of a future—where they're not just mere words—
but a force to be reckoned with in this tumultuous world.

The woman whose life is in danger of death
will not be silenced; she'll continue to rise.
She knows that her voice, her pen, and her very breath
have the power to change the world and make the future bright.

ANILA BUKHARI

Moon Beauty

I'm a lover of the moon
who sees me in my weeping and my swoon.
In moments of solitude and within the crowd,
in times of sorrow, and while laughter is loud.

Moon, my accomplice through complication and strife,
you bring me solace in the darkest of nights,
and your gentle glow is a beacon in the darkness,
guiding me through every twist and turn.

I adore your radiant beauty
and the stars that twinkle in your celestial abode.
You light the path for all without a care;
for those who need your glow—you are always there.

Oh moon, you teach me lessons so profound
to hide from people who don't want to be found,
to be with individuals who embrace your gentle light,
and to be a guiding star in the darkest of nights.

DAUGHTER'S NOT A CURSE

How wondrous is your presence!
You care for us, even in the depths of night.
Your luminous charm brings us peace,
a respite from the chaos, a moment's release.

Moon, you are a gift to behold,
a celestial wonder, always untold.
In the vast expanse of the night sky,
you shine with grace, never asking why.

So, I declare my love for you, moon,
for you give me hope dispelling all fear.
In your embrace, I find solace and peace.
A lover of the moon, my love will never cease.

ANILA BUKHARI

Day of Judgement

Oh, the fleeting nature of lifestyles,
how swiftly it passes us,
like grains of sand slipping through our palms,
and leaving us with the most effective memories to preserve.

In our pursuit of pleasure and satisfaction,
we overlook the fragility of our lifestyles.
We are engulfed in trivial interests and distractions,
and are blinded to the beauty that surrounds us.

Days slip away like whispers in the wind.
Moments are lost in the abyss of time.
We chase after dreams and goals,
never knowing the brevity of our top.

Sorrow comes knocking at our door,
a stark reminder of existence's transience.
In its grip, we weep and mourn
for the moments we took with no consideration.

Why do we stay on what we lack
when we've got so much to be pleased about?
It is the character of humanity, it seems,
to constantly yearn for what lies past our reach.

Yet, in the future, we shall depart this earthly realm—
leaving behind all that we hold precious.
Our lives are but a temporary rent,
and the Day of Judgment is close, too.

Oh, how foolish and careless we are,
lost in the slumber of ignorance,
and engrossed in worldly interests,
and forgetting our souls' real importance.

Awaken, oh stressed soul, wake up!
Let no longer existence's fleeting nature pass you by,
Embrace religion and start seeking for eternal truths,
before the sands of time ultimately run dry.

ANILA BUKHARI

God is Always with You

Think positively, my dear.
Ignore the horrific things; let go of the worry.
Hate may hit hard, but remember this, my friend:
God is always with you until the very end.

When peace eludes you through riches or apparel—
listen closely, for God's calling is higher.
He loves you more than you could ever conceive.
Even in your tears, he's there to relieve.

No matter the hour, wherever you may be,
don't hurt the hearts of those whom you can see.
This world is God's dwelling, a sacred place;
where love and compassion should always be embraced.

As snow blankets the earth on a wintry night,
I sit with my cat; no one else is in sight.
With books open in my hands, seeking solace and peace,
I hear a voice calling me, urging me to release.

A voice that speaks of humanity's plight,
prompting me to act with all my might.
When I witness a puppy shivering in the cold,
my heart yearns to embrace, to help unfold.

DAUGHTER'S NOT A CURSE

Spread peace and kindness far and wide,
and be a beacon of light in this world, there by your side.
For the voice that calls me is God's own grace—
guiding me to live with love and embrace.

So let us think positively—forget the hate,
and remember God's love is never too late.
In moments of solitude, with our faithful lion,
let's answer that calling with actions divine.

For in the act of spreading peace and care,
we discover a purpose beyond what is rare.
In a world that is longing for love's warm touch,
let us be the ones who give so much.

ANILA BUKHARI

I Lost My Heart

I misplaced my peace when I cared about what they would say,
when their words held power, I would lose my way.
My energy tired while the thought of losing loomed,
as self-doubt consumed me, my dreams were entombed.

I misplaced my heart to whispers behind my back,
the words of friends and loved ones, an attack.
Their reactions and actions brought tears to my eyes,
Aching wounds inflicted, heartrending cries.

But now, I am wise, for I have learned to see;
that others' love or hate does not define me.
My focus has shifted; my priorities—clear;
to love my God and humanity, nothing to fear.

In this vast tapestry of gender and belief,
I find peace and love, granting me relief.
The price of living is shedding the weight
of negativity that hindered—and sealed my fate.

So, I ignore the naysayers, their words I dismiss,
and listen to the voice of my guide, my compass.
With kindness as my guide, I will forge a new way,
free from the shackles of what others might say.

For in this world, to truly live and be free,
we must bury the negatives—let our spirits be.
Let love and compassion be our legacy,

Memories

I take a seat with my grandmother—a beloved embrace.
Drinking coffee, our souls intertwine;
as the moon's gentle glow provides a divine contact.

Her fingers—a haven in which shut-eye abounds.
Her love, a refuge, so pure and profound.
Though years have slipped by since she passed away,
her presence still lingers in where memories play.

Oh, how I long to experience her soft touch,
to hear her testimonies, her knowledge—so much.
In childhood's embrace, I could not conceive—
the individuals who would die or those who might live.

For love is aware of no bounds; it knows no divide.
It is the light in the darkness, the anchor that guides.
And although she's departed, her love remains real;
a beacon of warmth in all that I do.

I emit her laughter, her soothing voice,
the consolation she introduced; was a gift, not a choice.
But in the depths of my heart, her spirit's alive—
forever loved in a place that love cannot hide.

So, allow the rainfall, allow the moon softly gleam,
in my grandmother's fingers, I'll forever dream.
For in that sacred space, love's essence blooms,
and I'm reminded of lifestyle's sweetest plumes.

ANILA BUKHARI

Thank You, God

Thank you, God, for the pain I've endured,
for the challenges that tested and made me strong,
through every struggle, I found my voice—
you shaped me—molded me all along.

Thank you, my pain: you've taught me well—
to rise above and stand tall as a leader.
You propelled me forward—fueled my fire;
in your presence, I became a believer.

And to all my haters, I express my gratitude;
for your doubt and disdain, I owe you a debt.
You've ignited a passion within,
and through your negativity—I've found my asset.

Thank you, rejecters, for your scornful gaze—
in your hatred, I've found self-acceptance.
You've shown me the power of resilience,
and through your disbelief, I've discovered my own essence.

I'm grateful for every breath I take,
for the taste of life upon my tongue;
the cool breeze that whispers in my ear,
reminds me that every moment can be sung.

For this life I've been given, I'm truly blessed,
a chance to change, to break barriers and walls,

So, thank you, God, for the pain that's shaped me;
for the haters and rejecters that have tried.
In gratitude, I find strength and purpose,
to live this life, unafraid, with arms open wide.

Believe

Yes, I believe in myself, even though doubts might also come my way.
People question my abilities, but I will not be swayed.
I accept myself as who I am, with all my flaws and glory.
Why should unhappiness consume me when I know my own story?

People often misunderstand, misjudge, and misconstrue,
but I refuse to let their ignorance define what I can do.
In this dark night, I am a shining star, bright and bold,
a ray of hope in a world that often feels cold.

Yes, I believe in myself, in my strengths, and in my worth;
all my grief, sorrow, and fears dissipate, losing their berth.
For I am human, created with beauty, kindness, and purity,
I do not care for the opinions of others or their scrutiny.

Let them think what they will, those haters and their disdain,
I rise above their negativity, judgments, and pain.
For I believe in myself, in the depths of my soul's core,
and that belief is all I need always and forevermore.

ANILA BUKHARI

Black Women

Black women; radiant and ambitious,
their stories, ready to be told.

Why, dear ones, do you doubt your worth—
when your beauty shines upon this earth?
Why do you question the shade you wear—
when black is a color beyond compare?

In a world that casts shadows of doubt,
blackness stands tall, unwavering—devout.
It carries the weight of a thousand stars,
a testament to resilience that leaves no scars.

Oh, the nights that have witnessed your tears,
the struggles endured throughout the years.
White and brown mocking, with unkind voices,
but know, dear sisters, they are blind choices.

For they overlook the history deep,
the champions who fought, who dared to leap.
Muhammad Ali, the boxing king,
Maya Angelou, whose words still sing.

DAUGHTER'S NOT A CURSE

And let us not forget Mandela's might,
a beacon of hope, a guiding light.
These icons—they wore the same color,
and their legacies, in blackness, were laid.

So, black women, embrace the night,
for within it, your beauty takes flight.
You are more than the color you don,
a symphony of strength—forever strong.

No more doubting, no more despair—
in every step, know that you're rare.
Black women: stand tall, proud, and true—
for the world needs your beauty—through and through.

True Happiness

In search of genuine happiness, I wander
a country of mind misunderstood by all.
For humans crave what they deem as pleasure;
in possessions, partners, friends, or dreamlike places.

But happiness, dear souls, hides deep within—
within the caverns of your mind and heart.
Not found in fleeting desires, dreams, unfulfilled,
but in acceptance of every aspect of life.

Reflect, my friends, on this profound truth,
That happiness eludes those who seek,
For desiring a partner, gaining a mate,
Brings fleeting joy, a momentary glimpse.

True happiness—not a brief glimmer,
is found in accepting life's blessed embrace;
with all its ups and downs, its joys and pains.
In gratitude, we find true solace and grace.

So, pause and ponder—for it is not in things,
in fulfilling dreams, where happiness thrives.
But, in accepting which you have been blessed
and embracing what you lack—your soul shall thrive.

Unveil the veil of misunderstanding, my friends,
and let true happiness fill your being—
for it resides not in external achievements,
but in surrendering and simply being.

Open your hearts—let go of the chase,
and feel the bliss of life in its every shade.
For in acceptance lies the key to lasting joy.
In embracing all, finding true happiness.

A Painful Moment

A painful moment shattering her heart's glow.
Her daughter—lost before her very eyes,
leaving her broken and her spirit capsized.

She yearns to feel the presence that once was there,
she kisses the clothes her daughter used to wear.
The fragrance of perfume, a delicate reminder
of a love so pure, a bond no distance can hinder.

She clings to her memories, with tears on her cheek,
kissing the clothes her daughter used to search for.
A picture in her pocket, a reminder held tight.
Every year, on her birthday, she weeps through the night.

No distance can sever the affection they share,
united forever, their souls on a celestial stair.
Though they are apart, their connection remains
in the realm of love—their bond, forever sustains.

On the anniversary of her daughter's death,
she hugs the cold grave where her spirit lies.
Whispering words of love to the heavens high,
knowing their love transcends beyond the sky.

For a daughter's mother, distance holds no sway,
their love unites and shines brighter each day.
Though they will not share the same earthly space,
their love dances freely in an eternal embrace.

ANILA BUKHARI

Morning Light

In the early morning, as the sun rises,
awaken to a world of endless skies.
Forgiving what has been lost—a gentle release,
embrace the present, and find inner peace.

Divide your morning; a routine so sweet,
with meditation—a tranquil retreat.
Allow your thoughts to wander and roam;
find solace in this sacred space called home.

Next, embark on a journey to explore a new language,
expand your thoughts, and let knowledge burn.
With words and terms, a tapestry unfurled,
discover new worlds, and let knowledge be shared.

Yoga beckons with its graceful embrace;
stretch and bend, and discover harmony and grace.
Through each pose, the body awakens
a dance of energy, a soul that shakes.

DAUGHTER'S NOT A CURSE

Prayers softly whispered, a connection profound—
to a higher power, sheer silence surrounds.
With gratitude, we offer our thanks.
For this precious life and every rank.

Within this morning, the key is found—
the spice of life, and the flavors abound.
To awaken early, to greet the dawn,
is to embrace life—to carry on.

For in this morning routine so dear,
lies the power to overcome every fear.
To forgive, to learn, to seek, and to find,
a morning routine, a gift one of a kind.

So rise with the sun, let your spirit soar,
embrace the morning, forevermore.
In this dance of routines, let your heart be seen,
for in the morning light, you are truly serene.

ANILA BUKHARI

My Soul's Secret

In the depths of my being, secrets and techniques reside,
unknown to my body—where they hide.
Deep as the ocean, my soul holds true,
revealing the mysteries that only it knew.

Within the recesses of my spirit's space,
wounds shall heal, and pain—transform to grace.
A metamorphosis: where darkness finds light,
emerging from turmoil shining ever so bright.

Those who harmed, rejected, and despised—
gifted me hope like a sparkling surprise.
They ignited a fire—fueled my energy,
for their actions unveiled my inner synergy.

For every harm endured, a lesson was learned;
from every rejection, resilience was earned.
The hatred they harbored transformed within me—
into strength and compassion for all to see.

My soul's secret, a guide through life's strife,
transforming all wounds, transmuting to life.
With every trial endured, a diamond's gleam,
a testament to the power within my soul's stream.

In the depths of my being, secrets unfold,
revealing the stories that were once, untold.
Through pain and rejection, I find my way,
transforming all darkness into a brighter day.

About the Author
Anila Bukhari

Anila Bukhari emerges as a luminous thread in the legacy of Pakistan, weaving tales of empowerment. A beacon of hope in a world shrouded in adversity, she stands as the epitome of courage and conviction as she etches her mark on the annals of history.

Anila, the daughter of the nation, embodies the essence of strength and purpose. She wielded the pen as her sword from the tender age of ten, crafting prose infused with the fervor of change. In a society veiled by patriarchal norms, she dared to challenge the status quo while amplifying the voices of the marginalized and disenfranchised.

With each stroke of Anila's pen, she paints portraits of courage and defiance while shedding light on the harrowing realities of child marriage, forced unions, and plights of the orphaned. In her literary opuses, *No More Tears* and *Whispers of the Heart*, she weaves a tapestry of awareness and ignites conversations that reverberate across continents.

Anila's journey continues to transcend the field of literature and is an example of activism and a harbinger of change. At the tender age of fourteen, she started a crusade for peace and dedicated eight years of her life to the noble cause. Her efforts have culminated in international acclaim and bestowed her works with the prestigious international Excellence Community Service Award, an ink-filled testament to her unwavering commitment to humanity.

Anila's endeavors extend beyond the written word. She is a catalyst for action and change. Through her initiative, *No More Brides, Just Shine,* she wages war against the scourge of child marriage, mobilizing communities and igniting a spark of hope in the hearts of the oppressed. From organizing speech competitions to spearheading educational campaigns, she leaves an indelible mark on the landscape of advocacy.

Amidst her tireless crusade, Anila remains grounded in compassion and extends a helping hand to those in need. Through her project, *Hopeful Hugs,* she brings solace to homeless children and cancer patients, embodying the true essence of altruism.

Anila Bukhari, a visionary in her own right, is not merely a writer and activist. She is also a testament to the indomitable spirit of the human soul. Inspired by the timeless wisdom of Rumi, Maya Angelou, and Khalil Gibran, she dreams of a world emancipated from the shackles of injustice. A world where every girl can aspire to greatness.

In the hallowed halls of art galleries in the USA, Florida, and the Philippines; her verses adorn the walls, hanging as a testament to her transcendent talent. Her words resonate in the hearts of millions, a clarion call for change in a world yearning for transformation.

In her, we find the embodiment of beauty with brains, intellect, and compassion—a true luminary whose brilliance knows no bounds. Anila Bukhari, the daughter of the nation, is a force to be reckoned with and a guiding light of hope for generations to come.

About the Editor

Brandy Lane

Brandy Lane has lived most of her life in Indiana and Colorado. She published her first book, *Where Beautiful Loves*, in December 2020 under her imprint **Where Beautiful Inks**. Just after the release of her first book, she discovered anthologies as an option for publishing and has since had poetry pieces included in over three dozen publications. These publications include *Poetry 365 by RDW* (both abridged and unabridged editions) for November, December, January, February, March, April, May, and June, and special editions of *Creator*, and *Self Portrait*. Red Penguin Books has published her pieces in *'Tis the Season's*, *The Flower Shop on the Corner*, and *The Ocean Waves*, as well as *Bloom*, their magazine. Clarendon House Publications published her poems in their *Poetica 2* and *Poetica 3* anthologies and her work was also included in Ink Gladiator's Press anthologies of *The Rise and Fall of Chimera's* and *Gray, We Hide our Colors Within* and *Uncaging the Phoenix*. Indie Blu(e) Publishing published a mental health piece in *Through the Looking Glass: Reflecting on Madness and Chaos Within* and their newest anthology, *But You Don't Look Sick*. 300 South Media Group has published her in *As Darkness Falls*, *Shadow of the Soul*, and features her first flash fiction piece in *Sunset Rain*. Train River Poetry has published her in *Poetry 7*. She also appears in *Who's Who of Emerging Writers* by Sweetycat Press. In 2022, she was published by *Harness Magazine* in their November issue and Silent Spark Press' in *Amazing Poetry*. In 2023, she published three new poetry collections: *The Briny Sea of Poetry*, *Talking to the Moon*, and *Unrequited*. She also published her first anthology, *Winter: A Poetic Anthology* featuring 25 poets worldwide. In 2024, she is included in *The Caryx Collective* by Pendraig and *Ovation* by Jimmy Broccoli. Brandy has also published another collection of poetry, *Where Beautiful Loves II*, and another anthology, *Love Is Pain*, and is working diligently to produce several more.

Becoming well-known for her abilities in her poetry community, she has started collaborating with other poets to help their voices be heard. Anila Bukhari is the first of whom Brandy hopes to be a burgeoning group of authors to be published under her imprint of **Where Beautiful Inks.**

Brandy can be found online on Instagram and Facebook @wherebeautifullives.

About the Associate Editor

Kelsey Annin

Kelsey Annin was born and raised in Greenville, South Carolina, where she resides with her amazing family. She has an incredibly supportive husband and two beautiful and extremely active boys. She thanks God every day for her blessings and couldn't have asked for a better family.

Kelsey has been writing since grade school and has always found creativity to be therapeutic. She finds writing to be one of the most productive ways to release a range of emotions to help her deal with life and the relationships around her. She has aspirations to publish her own books in the future, including poetry and fiction novels.

Kelsey would like to dedicate a special thanks to her mother who has always been there to correct her grammar, encourage Kelsey in her creativity, and push Kelsey to her best ability. She always believed in Kelsey, and it is because of this that she has a deep love for creativity.

I escape expressively inside the pen when I need to feel awake again.

Exploring who I am, I dig up the voluptuous lion

underneath the humble lamb.

I am a wrestling warrior with ink stripes on my frenetic face.

I'm besoothed by a binding embrace as I swiftly sew the spine with grace.

Crying colors caught up in the pages with a nimble imagination untold.

I will not be silenced from myself as this sapient story unfolds.

~Kelsey Annin

Instagram: @whimsicalwisdoms_bykels

Other books by Where Beautiful Inks

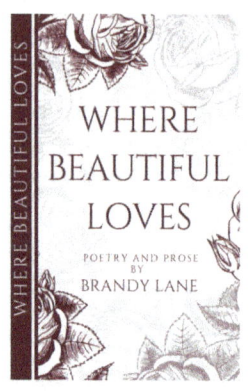
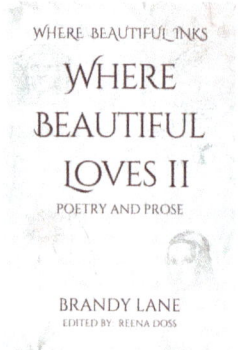

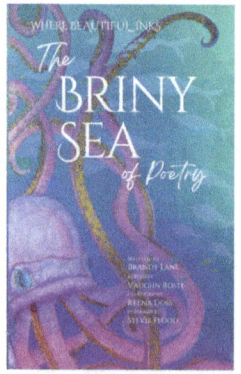

www.ingramcontent.com/pod-product-compliance
Lightning Source LLC
Chambersburg PA
CBHW050226100526
44585CB00017BA/2085